Survivors' Picnic

Poems by Debra Bruce

Word Press

Published by Word Press
P.O. Box 541106
Cincinnati, OH 45254-1106

ISBN: 9781936370993
LCCN: 2012952914

Poetry Editor: Kevin Walzer
Business Editor: Lori Jareo

Visit us on the web at www.word-press.com

Cover painting, "I Dreamed I Could Dance,"
by Suzanne Keith Loechl.

Survivors' Picnic

Acknowledgments

Grateful acknowledgment is made to the following publications in which these poems, sometimes in earlier versions, appeared:

Adanna: "12-Step Ballade"

The American Poetry Journal: "Swans Grooming"

The Atlantic: "Childhood," "Plunder"

Crab Orchard Review: "The Announcement"

Christian Science Monitor: "The Promise"

Columbia Poetry Review: "Birdwatcher"

The Cincinnati Review: "Warm Stone Massage"

Dark Horse: The Scottish American Poetry Journal: "Himself Again"

Escape Into Life: "Fabulous Avenue," "What It Leads To," "Two Fibs"

The Formalist: "Between Them"

Innisfree Poetry Journal: "Custody Haiku," "The Magician," "Stumbling Block"

Measure: A Review of Formal Poetry: "The Queen Is Meeting with the Union Reps," "Warm-Up in Charismatic Scales"

Mezzo Cammin: An Online Journal of Formal Poetry by

Women: "Arctic Caveat," "Ceremony," "Feminine Triolet," "A Notable Confession"

The National Poetry Review: "The Newcomer," "Note from an Extremophile"

Ploughshares: "At Large," "Necessary Magic"

Poetry: "Annual Survivors' Picnic," "Nervous Metaphors," "This Time Last Year," "The Unmothering"

Prairie Schooner: "Everything We Wanted," "Her Fiftieth Fall," "Hope," "Living with Your Diagnosis: A Few Tips," "Someone's Attention," "A Warning"

Shenandoah: "December's Gift," "Objects of Desire"

Southern Poetry Review: "Aerial View"

Valparaiso Poetry Review: "Women's Divorce Group"

The Virginia Quarterly Review: "So What," "Late Winter Lesson"

"The Unmothering" was reprinted in *Letters to the World* (Red Hen Press).

"A Notable Confession" was originally part of a collaborative sonnet sequence. The first line was written by Mary Agner.

Thanks to Elizabeth Johnson and Barbara Egel, first readers for several of these poems.

In memory of my father,
Willard Bruce

Table of Contents

I.

Warm Stone Massage

Down by the river stirred up kettle of sun,
heated stones in aromatic oil.
Oval on my navel, round in my hands,
rubbing my wrists, stubbed my wedding band.

Trouble at home, trouble in a body.
Roll on me, solar stones, but do not tell.
Calico, follow your motley down an alley.
Caterpillar, spit new threads for your bed of silk.

Stones rolled over my shoulders, scrubbed my scalp,
flickered down my backbone's pebbled strip.
What do I owe who whispering warmed the stones?
Body briefly untroubled in its home.

Summer choir loft, heady with heat, I prayed.
That's where I learned the word *indulgences*.
(Everything off except my wedding band.)
Roll on me stones, but don't tell anyone
how much I owe who made my riverbed.

This Time Last Year

Was it only last November
that you had to weigh two terrors,
choosing, going further
down a list from which to lose?
Well-intentioned friends assured you
that the giver gives us only
what he knows each one can handle.
Think it's true?

May your answer's distillations
spice the steeping, mulling weeks
left before what's bound to come.
May the lake you live near manage
all its grays without explaining.
May you meet each invitation
cheering you toward January
as you've learned to, by maintaining,
deep beneath a frozen surface,
expectations of the sun.

Someone's Attention

Decades ago you wrote, *Please be my muse,*
slipped your note into the scooped hip-pocket
of my jeans one day as I left class.
Later, the boy I loved who sat on the floor,
stretching his runner's legs from wall to wall,
waiting for me outside your office door,
would not have understood my fear.
He knew you by your jokes, your sparkling beard.
He leaned back humming with his headphones on.

A woman can't elasticize her years.
How right you were: when no one notices
as she walks by, when no one looks, it puts
a spin on spring. Now add a tinge of terror
to brighten things—ambiguous test results,
an empty house. But never mind.

You rubbed my neck; you asked me for my thoughts,
your touch pouring down my back a lavish wash
more confusing and more dangerous
than my lover shifting against that flimsy wall.
When he started whistling, you bristled,
and I turned to watch the door.
Whatever we said in the flustered seconds left,
neither of us was really listening.

Her Fiftieth Fall

When the sun's wan winnings
are revealed, it's no surprise up high,
but below,

the trees, in shocked denial, strip
to shrieks of light
in the glare of all that's bare.

Her would-be first insisted on kissing
with lips closed, but later
came the one for whom her body's
bouillon burst and she flung off
a tumult of scarves.

Will winter's low-impact pounding
outside her house be enough?
Might spring renew her sponsorship
at a more strenuous level?—matron
of March with matchsticks poised,

of all that smolders with what it knows,
of all that grovels,
even for a low-grade glow?

Between Them

He squirmed between them on the couch.
They talked above his head,
withholding words he shouldn't hear
or spelling them instead.

After they packed him off to bed
they thought they were alone.
But he pressed against his bedroom wall
and learned to read their tones,

standing almost as high as her waist,
to see, without being seen,
whether they leaned back, sandals off,
feet propped on magazines,

or sat up straight in separate chairs
while peaches in a braided bowl
took its pattern into their skin.
Which way would the summers go?

At Spirit Woods, he hiked between them,
suddenly shoulder-high.
No more exchanging looks—he read
their meaning, eye to eye.

They had a plan. They picked a trail.
They had a few years left
before the tumult of his words.
He listened, then raced ahead

to beat them to the waterfall,
to be the only one
who knew the news without being told
it's best for everyone,
fresh air hustling the trees, assessing
damage yet to be done.

Custody Haiku

His Dad's specialty—
charcoal-flamed chiliburger
followed by bad news.

Mouthful of gravel,
rock dropped in a hole, his Mom
squeezing his hand hard

as if to get tears
out of him. He wouldn't play
any of their games.

His room a gray pit.
She knocked all day, then slipped in
for dirty dishes.

His cellphone's smothered
metallic buzz—can't find it
or maybe he checks

then listens later
to Dad's brand-new chipper voice.
Delete. Or he checks

in his sleep, then rolls
away to stare at the wall
for a few more years.

A Warning

About that news flash from within
the new you, your *need to share* with me,
your now-at-last-released feelings flaring
until discretion's intricate crust erupts,
and from a deep core pour
all wrongs unnamed before;

you whose therapists and healing
gurus guarantee annealing
powers to words of molten
honesty, take note

of local casualty and who,
surviving, stays with you
as you breathe, relieved, the air
so changed, charged.

Annual Survivors' Picnic

She's so insistently chipper I hear
something militant in her cheer,
her chitchat's peppery pith:
You've got to just get over it. Lashed
by loss herself, did she hold on

so hard her suffering toughened
into this? Her hope's as brisk
an industry as cells crisscrossing
to cover horror; she packs
her upbeat stats, survival rates.

And sure enough, a full-blown June arrives
with stacks of paper plates—*Don't let the breeze
get these*—her pint of homemade relish—
Could you just pop this open please?—
its airtight tang released.

As sumptuous as another summer is,
why should I dwell? What's to worry about?
That all my green might be used up?
That my gold might never get out?

So What

The night of her news he made an exception—
letting his mother wrap herself around him,
holding on. OK. Enough.
But all along, despite that word, *survivor,*
flashing its high-fives, he knew, and stood apart—
hands in pockets, shoulders alert.
Spring hit on him, as it did the other kids.
All the more reason to crouch
inside the music in his pounding room,
so when they had to call him out,
he was prepared—everything
in there smashed—and he couldn't care less
whose job it was to clean up all the mess.

Plunder

Now that your surgery's
savagery's smoothed over
and the calm you've put on is balm
for all, and in the interstices
between catastrophes you find yourself
enjoying joy;
now that your *Why?*
is wisely subsiding, knowing no one
knows why one grows gold
slowly and one's bright green gets torched
overnight;

in this intensely present
tense, in its rush
of cherished perishables, you might splurge
skyward, spreading
your colors in a free fall
never dared before; or
with minimal fanfare slip
into the life you left, the least
predictable most delectable,
in whose midsummer noon you pop
a flip-top in thirst, and think…
and though you simply sip,
deeply drink.

Aerial View

Shot from her life not once but twice,
she slips her healthy body back on but can't quite fit
among those friends snug in their skins
who marvel in murmurs at her return,
who think that after such a flight, her drink
will always be spiked. It's true:
ennui's fake silks now slide right off her,
but up there

in the air, she preferred
her place below in a pack of groundlings—
ordering clothes from a catalogue,
searching for an herbalist to rub
a liniment so profoundly into her flesh
she was bound by heat to stay down.

She doesn't care if fear's rare air
affords a panoramic view.
Let daily errands run her around,
and if disaster asks her whereabouts
again, let's say we've seen her
everywhere but that she cannot be found.

Nervous Metaphors

Why would my oncologist put on
the uniform of those nameless cops
my father warned me about? *Always say,
"Hello Officer, nice day," then get away
as fast as you can.* And why not? He's armed

with news. And I'm stripped down to paper gown
and a heart beneath it pounding out of place.
He might as well stand in the hospital parking lot
as I roll in, his hand raised clearly: Stop,
my hair brushing my bare shoulder as I lean
his way in sun, *Nice warm day,*

isn't it? Not blurting, *Am I flying
toward my future too fast? Concealing contrabands
within?* while all around us trees withdraw
their green, preparing for a spectacle
of loss so brash I hold my breath.

When he lets me off with a warning, imagine how carefully
I cross the speed bump toward my getaway.
Do I appreciate such generosity?
Will I pay more attention now as leaf
by leaf, fall tears into the air,
its implications hurrying my way?

Living with Your Diagnosis: A Few Tips

Watch out—those *loved ones* might knock you down
to take it from you, hold it, shush it,
eyes wide with hope, then hand it back.

Never mind who walks away
as if there's nothing there.
It's easier after everyone forgets.

Let them believe *behind you*
instead of *everywhere* as you learn
to watch your step, shift your weight,
make room in all your plans.

The trick is not giving in to its constant demands,
even when you're at the kitchen sink,
ozone gusting through the window you shoved unstuck.

Pretend it isn't even on your radar.
Don't encourage it with direct attention
any more than you'd chat with an oncoming storm,
especially one with tendencies toward rotation.

Just keep putting those dishes away, matter-of-factly.
I never said you were going to love it, exactly.

II.

Childhood

Exiled once, allowed back in
to guide you through,
I didn't know my time was up.
But by the river, in snapping grass,
still in the habit of noticing,
crouching with you at a leaf or wing,
I spotted caterpillar frass
speckling milkweed as he feasted,
getting ready to split, released
from a too-tight self. In just a week
he'd grow a better, brasher skin.
Exiled once, allowed back in,
I leaned down in the snapping grass,
but stopped at the thud of your new voice:
Come on. Big deal. So what.

Everything We Wanted

Grande rhumba frappuccino—
double-shot to jump start hearts.
Jet streams have released June weather
fully loaded with our pleasures.

Kids dropped off in color-coded
campshirts under summer trees—
high-fives, headcounts, no one's missing.
Someone's mom waves when she sees

someone else's mom she meant to
call back, call me when you can,
promise, listen, talk, let's try to—
doors slid shut on minivans.

Rush-hour crush begins to loosen,
injured lifted off, lanes merged.
Someone's weekly grief group's meeting—
first names only, speak the words

no one speaks to sister, mother,
husband, lover's raging child.
Someone's hand on someone's shoulder
warms it for a minute.

At Large

Was his anguish the squeeze of strangers
ravaging *his* language?
How did his anger strangle,
then snap him free at twenty-one to choose
a certain neighborhood in the city
for revenge, *carnage,* and split the scene
with a new name, *gunman,*
lavished on him by newsmen as he crossed
state lines, tuning in?

All we knew was three days
when the sun had the park to itself,
summer thunderheads advancing
harmlessly above open space
while we kept our kids inside,
while politicians' *Why?*
and *Why?* rose up the spiral in a shell.

The gunman had nothing to tell.
Gathering speed, bearing
down on all the facts,
he turned the weapon on himself.

Necessary Magic

Just give me a second to leap
from your path each time your need
to run me down speeds up,
your just-hit-thirteen, split-second
shattered-glass brilliance
spilled. I've had to extricate you

from yourself, to hoard each shard
of hope, refusing
your oceanic effusions, to find
an inland calm where I can slowly wind
the winds around my hands,
and think. But not for long.

Even grown Achilles soaked
his sulking plea until his mother
shot from the sea and promised
to plunge the surf and rise
to the highest, most dangerous gods

to save her child. Whatever you just muttered
under your breath—even as I crumble,
I reassemble. Even as I speak to you
inches from the door that won't let me in,
I'm oiling all my muscles before I swim.

What It Leads To

I met him the summer I turned thirteen—
shipwrecked Odysseus,
naked, caked in brine, embarrassed
by a sunditzed maiden's presence.

Watching him wash and wrap in fleece,
wipe grit from his golden flask,
I would have bathed him in olive oil
myself if he had asked.

I lay across chenille to read
while my sisters sizzled outside,
my dripping one-piece on the floor,
the knotty pine all eyes.

A girl who fell in love with a stream
got bedded under a wave.
My mother's vacuum nosed my door
and thumped as if to say

she knew what was going on in there,
this was her final warning.
My night for dishes was every night,
and then I read till morning.

Who Needs a Language Anyway?

She says she's never going to France.
She's nothing like her older sister
and tells her so, so just shut up.
There's no one to talk to anyway

unless you're like her older sister,
snobbily burbling French syllables,
but no one's listening anyway.
All summer in the crowded humid house

she's snobbily burbling French syllables,
clueless about making travel plans
to escape the crowded humid house.
Meanwhile, a tent is pitched in their yard

as if to announce its travel plans
to nowhere: 14 and under, go free,
into the tent pitched in the yard.
The younger sister can handle things

out there, almost 14, and free.
She knows that no one's noticing
the zipped-up tent. She can handle things
even if her boyfriend is 19

and knows that no one's noticing.
Morning runs the dew off the grass.
So what if her boyfriend is 19—
book learning isn't everything.

When morning runs the dew off the grass
he'll be gone, so just shut up.
Book learning isn't everything.
She says she's never going to France.

12-Step Ballade

It bugs you how that redhead clangs.
Why can't she just get over it?
Why would I think you'd ever join
a club with such a membership?
You're fine—I know—you toss a quip,
just missing me. It slits the air.
In case you ever want some help,
on Tuesday nights they're always there.

According to you, there's nothing wrong.
My mind's meringued with pop-psych crap—
storming fathers, sons gone wrong.
You did your time on a mountaintop.
A pent-up horse inflamed your hip.
An accident turned you to prayer
and Jesus—but then you gave him the slip.
On Tuesday nights there's someone there.

I'd rather not have to watch again
when you pull a knife and slowly step
toward someone who mispronounced your name,
then end up slicing your fingertip.
A girl took off her sock and wrapped
your hand in stripes while you glared
as if you'd been unjustly slapped.
On Tuesday nights they're always there,

even if you make things up,
don't tell where you hid below the stairs,
your name called out—a thunderclap.
On Tuesday nights they're always there.

The Unmothering

Because her absence is now a presence
wherever you go, although it's true she never
approved of what you live by,
knew what you're most moved by;
because you are as capable as she
was culpable, you now consider dropping
all charges against her, notwithstanding
the decades it took to make
an impeccable case.

Who among us has not been summoned
to watch you, at seven, spiral
in terror down cellar stairs, hurrying
to heave into her arms with a fact
you couldn't unlearn?
But she kept on ironing even while you pleaded:
Does everybody really have to die?

Whatever kept her from looking at you,
from touching you whose wingbeats
backed you harder and harder away
from her until you were trapped
against the wall—it's time
to let it go—her shoulders rounded down
as she smoothed over surfaces, folding, closing
herself around what would not, could not fly.

Himself Again

Because he left but didn't go,
she'll never prove there was a loss.
His presence pressured her to hope.
Her grief was an abandonment.

Papers were signed, forcing him
into a room she'd never seen.
She gave her name at guarded doors
to sit with someone who wasn't there.

Still, at the news of his release
the air got bright inside her head
and sent her speeding down August roads
overcome by goldenrod.

She put the chairs back on the deck
and made her mind up to rejoice
with whoever he was, his safe return.
Summer wasn't over yet,

as witnessed by cicadas, that year's
miniscule administrators
of death unmarked by document,
or anyone's acknowledgment.

The Magician

You wouldn't believe it! One minute
he's just my husband, soaping a dish,

but when he turns to me, lifting a towel,
I have something to tell you—presto!

My chest is a cavity filling with crushed ice,
the air a shattered windshield I haven't even hit

yet as he steers me over familiar hardwood
to the couch.

      How did he do it?
I stared down hypnotized by our braided rug circling

and circling, as it had all these years.
And then it disappeared.

December's Gift

By shrill decree, as the wind
wills, fall's
bequeathing, brooding
beauty is arrested
in crisp bequest. It costs

a fortune to heat the house
in which the child
no longer roams in rooms
festooned with hope.

So why fribble with ribbons
another year? Why struggle
to unsnag those ancient lights?

The arrogance from suffering
in which you bask, insufferable
to yourself, might pass; even you

melt through,
your record lows notwithstanding,
your starkest days to date
which January waits to laminate.

Warm-Up in Charismatic Scales
for Tim, choir director

I never meant to be a follower.
How could someone drop everything and take off?
How could the ancients possibly have believed
bees honeycombed the infant prophet's lips?

I'd never drop everything and take off
for your heat-seeking glance, your repertoire of looks,
not for the honeyed infant prophet's lips.
A sleeper's soul can't fly off as a bird.

Your heat-seeking glance, your repertoire of looks
kept us alert as you swooped across the scales,
as if a soul might slip out in our song,
never to return. *Sleeper, wake up,*

be on alert. You swooped across the scales
to find the notes a soul might recognize
and be returned. You cued us, woke us up,
a thoughtful tongue decoding a honeycomb

to find the notes a soul might recognize.
The moans of mourning doves can be consoling,
a flute intoning, decoding the honeycomb.
We stepped into the air but felt no fear,

finding the moans of mourning doves consoling.
We climbed the notes like chimes of chandeliers.
You urged us into the air. We did not fear
the palpitation of wingbeats in our ears.

Climbing among a sky of chandeliers,
my only fear was that you'd leave us there,
the palpitation of wingbeats in our ears.
(They needed him. They trailed him everywhere.)
I never meant to be a follower.

The Promise

How do these birds survive the bleakness of winter?
    Naturalist Newsletter

Lie down, fiery ground.
But remember your embers and nudge
their buried lights when winter's white denies
I'm still around.
Cached seed, I know your whereabouts
in pinecone scale, know when to strip and pry.
Dried berries bristling
by snow-blocked road, my delicacy,
churn my body heat to round
my plumage for storage, expansive and patient.

Consider what you've heard.
Wings pulled in by wind-break shrub,
I'm undeterred.

III.

A Long Marriage

The hostages were released from Iran
on our small screen as we dined on the floor.
We could barely afford our wedding rings.
Tomorrow I'm selling mine—cash for gold.

In that era of quiche, we dined on the floor.
Tomorrow we meet to finalize.
Everyone's doing it—*cash for gold!*
The hostages filed back into their lives.

Tomorrow we meet to finalize
that we are no longer the audience
for the story of each other's lives—
a joke one winter, homemade crepes.

I am no longer the audience
for your midnight mountains of pork-fried rice
that followed the era of homemade crepes
and fed us through two more presidents.

Over midnight mountains of pork-fried rice
we planned, we traded our pleasures up.
On TV we watched our president
making jokes about his mistakes.

We traded all our pleasures up.
We could barely afford our wedding rings.
A president joked about his mistakes.
The hostages were all released.

Women's Divorce Group

She claims her ex was a filament of a man.
She's just met—online—a monument of a man.

Our red flags sprout. Watch out! Don't overcorrect!
Does he honor her independence—this brand new
man?

Does he know her favorite drink's an Irish car bomb?
And who is *his* government—this powerful man?

One woman draws her sari over her arm.
She says she's done with them—who needs a man?

Another bends toward her fistful of tissue shards.
Oh God—she's done it again—with the wrong kind of man.

We hoist her up. We scan each other's faces.
I refrain from admitting to them that I've met a man.

I'll slip off to meet him after our court adjourns,
relax in his paws—unrepentant—this warm and dangerous man.

Ceremony

I found a way to bring the rug upstairs.
I roll it up, then tug its heavy body.
I'm rearranging the rooms we used to share.

To slide it across the floor would take me years,
so I stand it up and let it lean on me,
shuffling with it toward the basement stairs.

Oh heavy mate—and who will greet me there?
—to usher in the new reality
of rearranging the rooms we used to share.

You wore a jacket I'd never seen you wear,
moving your things out, keeping your back to me.
I lose my grip, starting up the stairs,

but I don't fall. The rug slides down and flares
apart, away from me, deep burgundy.
I'm rearranging the rooms we used to share.

I don't know why I can't just leave it where
we stashed it away—for good, apparently.
I found a way to drag it back upstairs.
I'm rearranging the rooms we used to share.

Her Ex Sits Next to Her

It's far too soon for her to make a joke of it,
scuttle him away with a swish of wit,
This is a love seat, isn't it?

but too late to reach across the child-size space
between them, or look directly at his face.

Stumbling Block

A woman I once knew is now a man,
or on his way—though I still see her face,
the razzed-up haircut, earlobes that could wake
the masters of the centuries to collect
their colors, wet their brushtips and regard
such beauty as goes forth beneath the clouds,

or some such exhalation that could cloud
the summer of a girl becoming a man.
One drop of ice cream on her lip—regard
another man who stopped to scan her face
as if he'd found a portrait—shrewd collector—
of a banished girlish earl and hoped to wake

the art world up. My friend is lying awake
at dawn her first day back as *him.* No cloud
surrounding him, he hopes—he will collect
all queries, swift and forthwith as a man.
Whatever they think of him he's ready to face.
No reason he should drop in their regard.

Pop him with hellos, or disregard
the obviousness of his awakening?
Does anyone look right into his face?
Some keep their voices muted, in a cloud,
thinking about the woman who was this man,
as they glance down pretending to collect

paper clips from a magnet while they collect
themselves. They must stay wide-awake—
They practice saying his new name, regardless,
but stumble on the pronoun *he* for man.
They concentrate like kids who stare at a cloud
until it clarifies into a face.

Newcomers in his life won't have to face
him with such vigilance, recollecting
a woman they once knew, circling in clouds
of ambiguity, a place with no regard
for thumping on solid ground and waking up
in a world of this-or-thatness. He's a man.

He's now a man. The thought keeps me awake.
His voice collects a thickness like a cloud.
Regardless, I see her face.

Swans Grooming

Although their mirror is a murk
of pond-scum and they're too busy to look,
you're welcome to check for milk-flecks
of feather flicked off as they work,
their beauty's business open for all to see
who walk this early, before an Ozone Action day
alerts the summer air, then turns it off.

One extends a wing like a sleeve,
turning its head to inspect. One swivels
to plunge its bill into plumage and fritter it—a sound
like a thumb along a fine-toothed comb
about to lay the law down on the head
of a girl whose wet hair's lost its part
and who should have known better than to swim in there.

Fabulous Avenue

I cut across Fabulous Avenue
going home from the Russian produce mart.
In each new mansion a vacancy
is vaulted up to the highest floor,
to the highest bidder as prices fall.

The townhouse residents were ticked
when a fabulous rooftop blocked their sun
and solar-paneled it all to itself.
They cursed the alderman's kickback butt
and littered the esplanade with junk.

Blame it on Botticino marble tiles
gleaming in their barefoot cool
though no one's walked there without hard shoes.
The third floor Jacuzzi hasn't yet
spritzed anyone with its fabulous jets
or massaged the small of a well-toned back.

My shopping bag keeps chafing my arm,
ripe tomatoes—cheap and sweet.
I rest in the shade of a portico
grand and stately as Monticello.
Tonight I'm making dinner for friends.
We'll bitch and joke and make new plans
for the future of our fabulous land.

Birdwatcher

Let me be bleak and indiscreet,
my fiery throat traded for scorch
long ago, my journey north—mating,
mothering—done. I miss
my estrogen, engine I smashed
into palatial pleasures to make a wreck
of kings.
          Am I to believe
these rubies, mauves, a fanfare
of wingbeats in a tree as she flies out—
her Ladyship—are enough?
That I should nibble henceforward
on hope the crumbled eggshell I scattered
in my yard will boost her calcium?
A snarl of hair I tossed
from my brush for her nest
might be snatched up
on her filching spree
with stems and milkweed fluff?

What kind of ingrate am I,
my colors muted for fall, song chipped
into chits with no more melody,
that I would miss this day?
          Where would I be?

Arctic Caveat

Do not arouse the snowy owl
from mothering. You're not allowed.
The wind must transmit your request
through feathers on her face which hear
your surreptitious step.

She has no broth for whooping cough.
Her egg's no cure for alcohol
or any other ill that leads
a violator down a hall
to find a sleeping nest.

Her own chicks huddle in a hollow
of rock she scraped out with her talons.
Your visits here could be curtailed
at a whim of wind, a motion filed
against your freezing hands.

Don't touch her nestling's twig of leg,
record its yellow eyes and beak.
Your research questions must be scanned
on solar disk, on treeless land.
Down she swoops, she comes with news.

Don't tell her, she'll tell you.
And if you knew, what would you do?
Restore to bone lost mineral?
Make laughter less ephemeral?
Make one child well?

Note From An Extremophile

an organism found in environments considered uninhabitable

I know what flipped your heart, Diver—
a flicker of red in the Arctic dark
brought you kicking
into our bedding of layered salt
until you found us out—the odd
cod hiding in his folds

below the floe, solitude
in cubicles of ice, the molecular
make-do of each life abiding
for centuries, until now
as your ship shoves deeper into the melt
where ice can be cored, as trees can,

as if we've all been waiting
like bulbs packed with plans
to get our stories out there
into the sun, where you come from.

The Newcomer

Our summer pond was mulling its debris.
A fledgling warmed a nest, invitingly.
Her descant flew above our melody.

October. Time for trees to be relieved
of leaves, the new one sang. Some froze in place—
a zero-tolerance lockdown brilliance.

But change still came. Powers that be. Time to negotiate—
unthinkable new restrictions of winter light.

Feminine Triolet

A woman must face her mirror
each day and present her case.
Year after year after year,
a woman must face her mirror.
On behalf of spring, whose career
is a windstorm of willow-lashed waste,
a woman must face her mirror
each day and present her case.

The Queen Is Meeting with the Union Reps

The queen is meeting with the union reps.
She wore her horses down, then ordered more.
Two leather jackets mount the blustery steps,

predicting victory—gold bouillons kept
in private suites may be released, they've heard.
The queen is meeting with the union reps.

It's drizzling cold outside, their mikes hooked up,
but still their words are wind-scurred, hard to hear,
two leather jackets mounted on blustery steps.

They praise our sacrifice. We'll soon get checks.
Today's free hot dogs are grilling in the square.
The queen is meeting with the union reps.

No more sweet deals, no falling on her neck,
the heat of her hand—the way it was before
two leather jackets mounted the blustery steps.

You, with bits of candied ginger left
in your pocket from the time you went to her—
heads up. She's meeting with the union reps.
Two leather jackets mount the blustery steps.

The Announcement

Catherine of Aragon, widow of Arthur, married his younger brother, Henry VIII.

The Bishop's blessed many a low-waisted bell.
And to the church the living call.
She's betrothed by death to a boyish king.
And to the grave do summon all.

A woman studies with her body.
Her king's mouth tastes of muscat-fig.
For one plush prince four rockers will rock,
but the bud, unopened, drops.

Tuning a bell's laborious
and noisy, not melodious.
Her honeyed months to come are gone.
His Majesty dines alone.

Too much tin, a bell's too thin
and brittle, though its tones might charm
a king who listens, again, for news.
The infant's in her arms

but dies in days. She knows her error's
recorded, the plangent, frantic ringing
she cannot silence, nor rock one rocker
carved by order of her husband, the king.

Objects of Desire

Anne of Cleves, fourth wife of Henry VIII

Silk women, come. Embroiderers, bewitch
his Majesty as her portrait did.
Ladies, scurry her plainness into satin,
grosgrain, taffeta; turn back her belled sleeve
to a hint of undersleeve, scatter slashings
among her gold, her purple cloth before

the emissary's sycophant kiss cools
and the king's lips moisten the dull hand
of the one he will annul: Anne.
Because her hips aren't in on it,
according to reports, because she isn't fine
as select threads of saffron or sweet
with a slight burn of ginger, cinnamon.

Because the king won't live to taste
in cocoa undiscovered depths
of innuendo, the first vanilla unsheathed
in his land, set steeping
on his tongue. Who
will please him—six wives, two daughters,
one sickly son?
He will not hear another birth bell rung.

A Notable Confession

c. 1633

The infinite or *finite* mystery?
Your Holiness, I pray, please take your pick.
Let's play our little joke on history:
I, Galileo, am a heretic.
I rushed my spyglass up the golden stair,
my pride pumped up—to magnify x 10.
Seeing the tiny faithful cross the square,
far off, amazed the doge's silken men.

But then I watched the sky. I take it back.
My prison is a villa, gathered beans
promised by my daughter, white grapes just picked,
her letters pleading with me, *come, soon, please.*
Do I, an old man, renounce Copernicus?
Of course I do. Don't be ridiculous.

Late Winter Lesson

I liked the single-digit days.
I knew exactly where I stood.
Trailing my dog down frozen ruts,
our iron routine, I knew the drill.

Someone was digging someone out—
the heft of breath, no wasted words—
while snow compiled its evidence
that no one was going anywhere.

I liked my mind riveted
on one idea, a single fear.
A late-night jet sounded too close,
amplified in dense-packed air.

It screamed, as if with shattering news,
then landed safely, all on board
preoccupied and matter-of-fact.
If forced to leave, I could get back.

But now the ground's aroused
by warming ambiguities.
Ice grows a smoother skin.
Who walks unwary will be chagrined.
I've already fallen twice.

About the Author

Debra Bruce is the author of three previous books of poetry, Pure Daughter and Sudden Hunger, both from the University of Arkansas Press, and What Wind Will Do, from Miami University of Ohio. She has received awards from the National Endowment for the Arts, the Illinois Arts Council, the Poetry Society of America, and Poetry magazine. The poems in this book have been published widely in journals including The Atlantic, Poetry, and Prairie Schooner. Originally from Albany, New York, Debra lives in Chicago.

About the Artist

Suzanne Keith Loechl is originally from England and grew up in Virginia. She now lives in the flat, expansive landscape of Illinois. Loechl is an oil painter with a background in landscape architecture. Her work has been exhibited throughout the Midwest, including Woman Made Gallery and The Illinois Institute of Art in Chicago. Her inspiration is gleaned from seemingly commonplace aspects of the landscape, and observations of how people exist in these environments. She believes the land we live in to be strangely beautiful—yet enormously fragile.

CPSIA information can be obtained at www.ICGtesting.com
Printed in the USA
LVOW06s2034140813

347913LV00002B/445/P